Avacandia

Getting To Know...

Nature's Children

TIGERS

Bill Ivy

SCHOLASTIC INC.

New York Toronto London Auckland Sydney
Mexico City New Delhi Hong Kong Buenos Aires

Facts in Brief

Classification of the tiger

    Class: *Mammalia* (mammals)

    Order: *Carnivora* (carnivores)

    Family: *Felidae* (cat family)

    Genus: *Panthera*

    Species: *Panthera tigris*

World distribution. India, China, Indonesia.

Habitat. Varies widely. Tigers can survive almost any climate —hot or cold, dry or wet. Their only requirements are plenty of food and water and thick vegetation to provide cover when they hunt.

Distinctive physical characteristics. Reddish-orange to brownish-yellow fur, marked by black stripes and white patches; ruff or longer hair on some adult males; biggest member of the cat family.

Habits. Solitary; males mark territory with scent and by scratching; hunt mainly at night, usually searching out and stalking prey though they sometimes wait in ambush.

Published by Scholastic Inc.
90 Old Sherman Turnpike, Danbury, Connecticut 06816.

SCHOLASTIC and associated logos are trademarks of Scholastic Inc.

ISBN 0-7172-6690-7   Printed in the U.S.A.

Have you ever wondered . . .

why tigers have stripes?	page 5
if baby tigers like to play?	page 6
where tigers live?	page 9
which member of the cat family is the biggest?	page 12
if all tigers look the same?	page 15
if tigers have good eyesight?	page 16
what a tiger uses its whiskers for?	page 19
how big tigers may grow?	page 20
how many toes tigers have?	page 23
if tigers are good climbers?	page 23
if tigers can swim?	page 24
how tigers keep clean?	page 27
if tigers have big appetites?	page 28
if tigers are good runners?	page 32
when tigers hunt?	page 32
how big a tiger's territory is?	page 35
how a tiger marks its territory?	page 35
how tigers greet each other?	page 36
how many babies a mother tiger has?	page 39
what newborn tigers look like?	page 39
if tiger cubs grow quickly?	page 40
how tiger cubs learn to hunt?	page 43
when young tigers are ready to leave home?	page 44
Words To Know	page 47
Index	page 48

Everyone knows what a tiger looks like. Its bright orange coat and black stripes make it easy to identify.

Most of us will only ever see a tiger in a zoo, where its magnificent coat really stands out. Strange as it may seem, however, the bold pattern of the tiger's fur is not meant to attract admiring attention. On the contrary, it is actually designed to help the tiger blend in with its natural surroundings and stalk its prey unnoticed.

If you'd like to find out more about tigers and how they live, read on. You will surely agree with one of the most famous tigers that "they're grrrrreat!"

Fun and Games

Like most animal babies, tiger cubs love to play. They will probably snuggle up with mom for a nap after lunch, but before long they will be up and frisking about again. A good tussle or a game of peekaboo is always fun, and if the cubs get bored with that, there are butterflies to chase and bugs and beetles (not to mention each other's tails) to pounce at.

Meanwhile mom rests, seemingly unconcerned. You might even think she's asleep—but you'd be wrong. Just let one of the cubs move a step too far from her side and she will instantly call it back with a sharp grunt. The cub comes willingly. It will be a long time yet before these youngsters are ready to venture forth on their own.

A tiger mother raises her cubs alone.

Tiger Territory

You can find tigers living wild in parts of Russia, China, India and Indonesia. They are very hardy creatures, and can survive climates ranging from the hot, humid tropics to the cold, icy north. They may live in rain forests, dry woods, grasslands, swamps, marshes or snowy mountains. No matter where it makes its home, every tiger needs three things to survive: water, lots of food and enough thick vegetation to hide in while it stalks its prey.

Overleaf:
The Siberian tiger's thick coat helps keep it nice and warm, even in the snow.

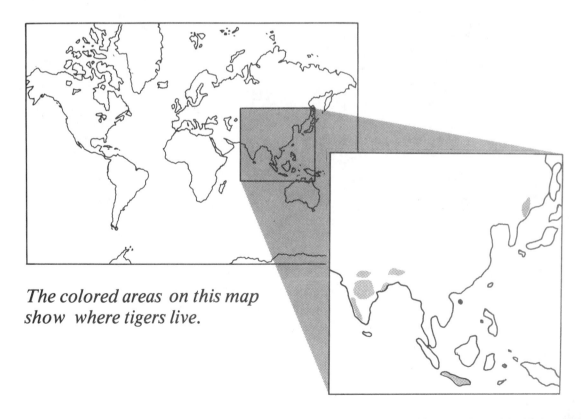

The colored areas on this map show where tigers live.

Big Cats and Little Cats

Tigers belong to the cat family, a family found all over the world. You may even have a member in your own home if you have a pet cat.

Zoologists divide all these cats into two groups: the big cats and the little cats. The little cats include house cats, lynx, bobcats, ocelots and cougars. Cougars? Don't those zoologists know how large cougars are? They do, but the distinction they make is between cats that roar and those that don't. Since cougars can't roar they don't qualify as biggies; tigers, lions, jaguars and leopards do.

And can you guess which one of these big cats is the biggest? Right—the tiger!

Now rare, the white tiger was once common in parts of India.

Tiger Types

There are several types of tigers and they differ in size and color depending on where they live.

The Siberian tiger of northern regions is the largest. It is yellowish in color and has an extra long, thick coat to protect it from the cold. It needs it! This tiger has to survive temperatures that drop as low as –45°C (–49°F). Brrr!

Tigers that live in the tropics, such as the Indian, South Chinese and Sumatran tigers, have shorter, thinner hair. These tigers also tend to be smaller and have more brightly colored fur.

A tiger's tongue is covered with short, sharp hooks that it uses to scrape every last bit of meat off a bone.

Tiger eye

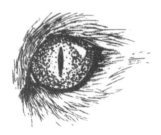

Cat eye

Tiger Eyes

One of the first things you notice about a tiger are its piercing, yellow eyes. And those eyes are as sharp as they look!

A tiger's eyesight is much better than ours, especially in very dim light. Like a great many animals, however, tigers are colorblind and see everything in shades of black, white and gray. This means that they may have trouble spotting an animal that's not moving, no matter how close it is, because it often blends in with its surroundings. But as soon as the animal makes the slightest movement—watch out!

A tiger's eyes react differently to bright light than your pet cat's do. If you look at a cat's eyes when it is outside on a sunny day, you will see that its pupils are narrow, black slits. However a tiger's pupils close down to tiny circles.

A tiger does most of its hunting at night but may continue during the day if it has not been successful.

More Super Senses

What seems like an almost silent forest to us can be alive with sounds to a tiger. Its large, cup-shaped ears help focus sound and make the tiger very sensitive to even the slightest rustle. You can find out how this works by cupping your hands and holding them behind your ears. Notice how much louder everything sounds?

While less important to its survival than its hearing, the tiger's sense of smell is also well developed. In addition, around the tiger's face are long, coarse whiskers that it uses as feelers. Almost as handy as a spare set of eyes, these whiskers help the tiger maneuver around twigs and branches even in the blackest night.

The tiger's long canine teeth are as sharp as daggers.

Heavyweights

Tigers are definitely BIG cats. Males may be 3 metres (11 feet) long from the tip of their nose to the tip of their tail and weigh 170 kilograms (400 pounds). One super-heavyweight tipped the scales at 293 kilograms (645 pounds). Tigresses are smaller, usually not much more than 2.5 metres (a little over 8 feet) in length, and they weigh in at about 135 kilograms (300 pounds).

Is it just a coincidence that the biggest tiger, the Siberian, lives in the coldest area? No. A bigger body tends to lose heat more slowly than a smaller one. The Siberian's size helps it to survive its cold climate.

Given its size and strength, it is no wonder the tiger has few enemies.

Quiet Feet

Despite their size, tigers are very light-footed and can move silently through any terrain. The large, rubbery pads on the soles of their feet and the fur between their toes help muffle any noise.

Claw retracted

Tigers have five furry toes on each front foot, but the "thumb" toe is a little higher up the leg and does not touch the ground. Their back feet do not have this fifth toe. Like all cats, tigers walk on their toes and the balls of their feet.

Claw extended

Tigers' paws are equipped with sharp, curved claws that are perfect for hunting. When not in use the claws are drawn back into protective sheaths. This keeps them from being worn down as the tiger walks over hard ground or rocks. When needed, the claws can be extended in the wink of an eye. Most cats also use their claws for climbing, but tigers are too heavy to be good climbers and rarely leave the ground.

While playing, tigers are usually careful to keep their claws drawn in.

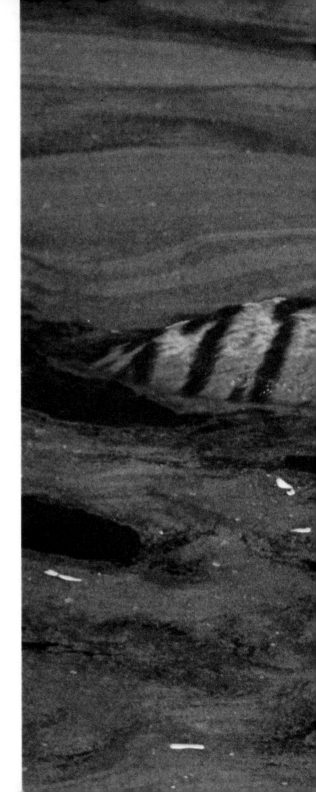

Cool Cats

All cats hate water, right? Wrong! Tigers love it and will often spend hours on a hot day just lying or standing in water to keep cool. They also find a quick dip very useful for cleaning insects and parasites out of their fur.

Because of their muscular shoulders and front legs, tigers are strong swimmers. Cubs learn to do the ''cat paddle'' while they are still quite young, and an adult can easily swim five kilometres or more (3–4 miles).

In the swim.

Looking Good

The tiger's striking reddish-orange or yellow fur is accented by jet black stripes and brilliant white markings. As well, many males have an attractive ruff of hair around their cheeks. Keeping such an elegant coat looking its best takes a lot of grooming, and the tiger spends a great deal of time each day licking itself clean.

Did you know that no two tigers look exactly alike? Each one has its own individual pattern of stripes that is as distinctive as your fingerprints. Even the markings on either side of a tiger's body do not match!

Even young tigers like to look their best.

Meat Eaters

Tigers eat meat and lots of it. They have enormous appetites and can eat up to 25 kilograms (55 pounds) at one meal. They average a good deal less than that over several days, however, and they often go for a week or more without eating anything.

Tigers prey mainly on deer, antelope and wild pigs, but they will eat almost anything that they can catch. This may be as small as frogs, turtles, fish and birds, or as large as water buffalo, elk, rhinoceros and elephant calves. When wild prey is scarce they may turn to an easy-to-catch meal of domestic cattle or goat.

Sometimes tigers swallow a few mouthfuls of grass and soil, probably to help in digestion.

Notice how the coat of this Bengal tiger helps it blend in with its surroundings.

An Undeserved Reputation

Tigers are shy and secretive, and they usually stay well away from human beings. Most will, in fact, run away if they catch sight of one. How then did tigers acquire their fearsome reputation as maneaters?

Tigers have been known to attack people on occasion. Usually it will be a mother protecting her cubs from someone who is getting too near her den. And sometimes it may be a tiger that is old or crippled or unable for some other reason to catch its normal prey. It may, for instance, have painful porcupine quills in its mouth, which not only make it irritable but make hunting game almost impossible.

Tigers are certainly dangerous, but they are not the deliberate maneaters that exaggerated stories would have you believe.

A tiger will normally drink several times during a meal.

On the Prowl

The black and orange hunter slinks silently through the forest. It carefully places each paw so that no sound will give it away. Pausing from time to time, it watches and listens. Then it continues its stalk.

Instead of searching out its prey, a tiger may try to ambush it—especially at water holes, where many animals gather. Whenever possible it will seek out an old, sick or lame animal that is not very fast. This big cat can only run quickly for about 25 metres (80 feet), so it must creep in very close before it attacks. Hunting at night helps it approach undetected.

Tigers are good hunters, but usually their prey is quick and gets away safely. The tiger knows there is no point in giving chase and simply moans quietly as it walks away frustrated. But when it is successful, probably only once in 15 or 20 tries, it lets out a victorious roar than can be heard a long way away!

Crouched and ready to pounce!

No Trespassing

Every tiger has its own territory where it lives and hunts. A male may share his domain with one or more females, but other males are not welcome and any bold enough to trespass are inviting trouble.

A tiger's territory may be about 65 square kilometres (25 square miles) if there is lots of food, or up to ten times that size if food is scarce. Obviously it is impossible for a tiger to guard all this land, so instead it regularly patrols its area and posts ''no trespassing'' signs. How? It scratches trees with its claws and scrapes the ground with its hind feet. And every so often it sprays the trees, rocks and bushes with its strong-smelling urine. These scrapes and scent markers let other tigers know that this property is spoken for. They may also allow male and female tigers to follow each other during the mating season.

On the prowl.

Getting Together

Tigers are loners and spend most of their lives by themselves. But if two tigers should meet, they will greet each other the way most cats do by touching cheeks or rubbing the sides of their bodies together. Once these formalities are over the two tigers go their separate ways.

The only time tigers come together is occasionally to share a meal or to mate. A male may follow a female's scent markings to locate her, or the two will roar back and forth until they find each other. If two males are interested in the same tigress they may fight, sometimes very fiercely. The female is not always impressed by these battles, however, and may end up choosing the loser or walking away from both of them!

Getting acquainted.

Cuddly Cubs

When the time comes for the mother tiger to give birth, she selects a suitable nursery. Tigers usually have a number of dens scattered throughout their territory, and the tigress will choose one that is well sheltered and close to water. She gives birth to anywhere from one to six babies, although the usual number is two or three. The cubs are about the size of small house cats and weigh around 1 kilogram (2 pounds). They are blind, helpless and totally dependent on their mother for care and protection.

Newborn tiger cubs spend most of their time drinking their mother's milk and sleeping. Their fluffy coats already show a striped pattern, and their feet seem much too large for their little bodies. It will be about two weeks before their eyes open and they get their first look at the world.

Growing Up

Tiger cubs grow very quickly. By the time they are six weeks old they may already weigh five times as much as they did at birth. Like all kittens, the cubs wrestle, tumble, stalk and snarl at each other. Sometimes the play can get quite rough, but it is just for fun and no one gets hurt.

By now these frisky youngsters are ready to leave their den for brief periods, and soon they will be venturing farther afield, tagging along close behind their mother. They keep track of her in the tall vegetation by following the white spots on the back of her ears. Should they lose sight of her they meow loudly.

When the cubs are about six months old they are ready to eat meat. While their mother is out hunting they stay hidden away in the den. But as soon as she returns they come bounding out to eat their dinner. The tigress waits to eat until all her cubs have finished.

If a tigress has to move her cubs before they are able to follow her, she will carry them one at a time by the scruff of the neck.

Lots to Learn

Before the young tigers can survive on their own, they have many important lessons to learn. First and foremost is the art of hunting.

The cubs were already preparing for this when they were playing and tumbling with their brothers and sisters. Now they watch their mother in action and begin sharpening their own skills by chasing after small game.

Becoming skillful hunters is difficult, and cubs may be hurt or even killed by their prey. It takes a lot of time and practice, and it will be well over a year and a half before the young tigers can effectively make their own kills. Their mother is very patient and helps them all she can.

Tigers in the wild may live to be fifteen years old.

Leaving Home

By one year of age the male cubs are almost as large as their mother and the females are just a little smaller. In another year or so they will be ready to leave their mother to make room for her next litter. Although adult tigers have few natural enemies, youngsters learning to get by on their own have to be wary of wild dogs, which may attack in packs.

Sometimes brothers and sisters remain together for a while before splitting up to find hunting grounds of their own. When they are three years old they are ready to seek out mates and start their own families.

Wild and Free

The human population of the world has grown enormously in this century, causing a serious problem for tigers. As more and more of their habitat has been turned into farmland, they have been pushed into ever smaller areas that can support them only in dwindling numbers.

Fortunately, things are beginning to look up for tigers. Countries where they live have passed laws to protect them and created reserves where they can live and hunt undisturbed. Maybe someday you will be lucky enough to visit one and see these beautiful animals prowling wild and free.

Until then, use your imagination. Picture a meadow at the edge of a dense forest. The last light of day is fading. Suddenly, unannounced by any sound, a tiger looms above the tall grass. Slowly, silently, its eyes shining in the semi-darkness, the huge cat advances . . . then stops. What is it? A sound? An odor? Something—for with a flick of its striped tail, the magnificent creature blends into the trees and swiftly, mysteriously disappears.

Words To Know

Cub Name for the young of various animals including the tiger.

Den Animal home.

Groom Brush or clean hair or fur.

Habitat The area or type of area in which an animal or plant naturally lives.

Litter Young animals born at the same time.

Mate To come together to produce young.

Parasite An animal or plant that grows and feeds on or in another one.

Pupil The opening in the center of the eye through which light enters.

Prey Animal that other animals hunt for food.

Ruff A collar-like growth of longer fur around the face of some animals, including some male tigers.

Territory Area that an animal or group of animals lives in and often defends from other animals of the same kind.

Tigress Female tiger.

Zoologist Scientist who studies animals.

INDEX

babies. *See* cubs

claws, 23, 35
climbing, 23
coat, 5, 15, 27
cubs, 6, 39, 40, 43, 44

den, 39
description, 5, 9, 19
diet, 28, 40
distribution, 9
  map, 9

ears, 19
enemies, 44
eyes, 16

family, 6
feet, 23
female, 6, 20, 35, 39, 40, 43

getting along, 6, 31, 36, 40, 44
growing up, 40, 43, 44

habitat, 9, 15, 46
hunting, 23, 28, 32, 43

lifespan, 43

locomotion, 23
male, 20, 35
mating, 35, 36

paws, 23
protection, 31, 35, 39

relatives, 12
roar, 12, 32

scent, 35
senses
  hearing, 19
  sight, 16
  smell, 19
  touch, 19
Siberian tiger, 15, 20
size, 12, 20, 44
strength, 31
stripes, 5, 27
survival, 9
swimming, 24

territory, 9, 35
types, 15

whiskers, 19

Cover Photo: Tony Stone Worldwide (Masterfile)

Photo Credits: Bill Ivy, pages 4, 17, 18, 21, 26, 33, 34, 45; Metro Toronto Zoo, pages 7, 10-11, 13, 14; Dennis DeMello (New York Zoological Society), page 8; Bill Meng (New York Zoological Society), page 22; ZEFA (Masterfile), page 25; Kamal Prasad (Valan Photos), page 29; Alan Wilkinson (Valan Photos), page 30; FPG International (Masterfile), page 37; Robert C. Simpson (Valan Photos), page 38; New York Zoological Society, page 41; Tony Stone Worldwide (Masterfile), page 42.

Getting To Know...

Nature's Children

GIRAFFES

Merebeth Switzer

SCHOLASTIC INC.

New York Toronto London Auckland Sydney
Mexico City New Delhi Hong Kong Buenos Aires

Facts in Brief

Classification of the giraffe

    Class: *Mammalia* (mammals)

    Order: *Artiodactyla* (cloven-hoofed mammals)

    Family: *Giraffidae*

    Genus: *Giraffa*

    Species: *Giraffa camelopardalis.* Nine subspecies.

World distribution. Africa, south of the Sahara.

Habitat. Open woodlands and tree-dotted grasslands.

Distinctive physical characteristics. Extremely long neck; long, thin legs with front ones longer than hind; short horns covered with skin and hair; mottled orange-brown and white-cream coat.

Habits. Band together in loose groups; most active in early morning and evening.

Diet. Leaves and twigs, especially of acacia, mimosa and wild apricot.

Published by Scholastic Inc.
90 Old Sherman Turnpike, Danbury, Connecticut 06816.

SCHOLASTIC and associated logos are trademarks of Scholastic Inc.

ISBN 0-7172-6690-7

Printed in the U.S.A.

Have you ever wondered . . .

when baby giraffes start to run and play?	page 6
if the giraffe has any relatives?	page 9
how tall giraffes can grow?	page 11
how many bones a giraffe has in its neck?	page 12
if giraffes ever fight with each other?	page 15
how well a giraffe can see?	page 18
how fast a giraffe can run?	page 21
if a giraffe has many enemies?	page 22
whether giraffes make any sounds?	page 25
what a giraffe does to show it is angry?	page 25
if all giraffes have horns?	page 26
if all giraffes look alike?	page 30
how long a giraffe's tongue can be?	page 33
how many teeth a giraffe has?	page 33
what giraffes eat?	page 34
how much giraffes eat?	page 34
if giraffes live alone or in groups?	page 38
if giraffes lie down to sleep?	page 38
how much a newborn giraffe weighs?	page 41
if young giraffes are playful?	page 45
how fast baby giraffes grow?	page 45
how long giraffes live?	page 46
Words To Know	page 47
Index	page 48

If you were an emperor living a few centuries ago and wanted to make friends with another emperor, what might you offer him as a gift? Gold? Rubies or diamonds? Fine silks? But most emperors already have those things. You want something even more rare and precious, something that will absolutely overwhelm that other emperor. How about a giraffe?

A giraffe! Yes, that is precisely what the Emperor of China chose some 500 years ago when he wanted a gift that would really impress the Emperor of India.

What is so special about a giraffe that it would be considered a gift for kings? Let's take a closer look at this gentle giant of the African plains and find out.

First Steps

Believe it or not, within a few minutes of its birth, a baby giraffe is struggling to its feet. It probably won't make it on the first try—after all it is no simple task to disentangle those long, spindly legs and figure out how to balance that long neck. But with some encouraging nudges and licks from its mother, the youngster will soon sort itself out and be reaching for its first drink of her rich, warm milk.

The young giraffe grows quickly. Within a few weeks it is ready to run and play and keep up with mom and the herd as they move across the plains in search of food. It has a lot to learn, but there will be time for fun too—for a quick romp or a short game of tag.

Keeping close to mom.

Giraffe Country

Scientists tell us that giraffe ancestors used to live in many parts of Africa, Asia and Europe. But that was millions of years ago. Today giraffes and their one living relative, the okapi, are found only in Africa.

The small, shy okapi makes its home in the dense forests of central Africa. Giraffes, on the other hand, live in open woodlands and on the tree-dotted savannas, or plains, where they can move about freely.

Opposite page: Given their great size, it is easy to understand why giraffes prefer wide open spaces to heavily wooded areas.

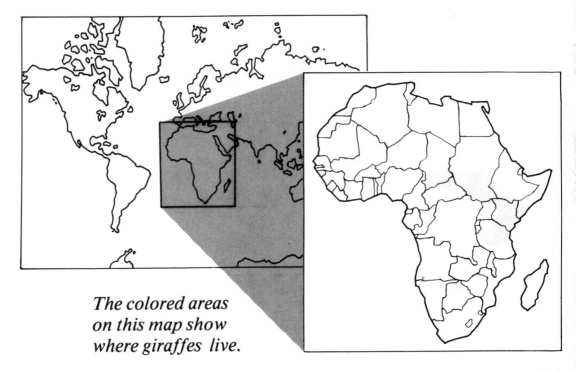

The colored areas on this map show where giraffes live.

Tall, Taller, Tallest

Although the elephant is considered the largest living land mammal because of its tremendous weight, the giraffe is certainly the tallest.

Male giraffes have been known to reach heights of close to six metres (20 feet). That is taller than many two-story houses! An average male, while not quite that tall, is still huge, and the dainty female, who is shorter yet, often tops 4.5 metres (15 feet).

Even a newborn giraffe may measure in at two metres (over 6 feet), which is taller than most adult men and women.

Because its front legs are longer than its hind legs, the giraffe's body makes one continuous slope from its horns to its tail.

"Going Up!"

What is the first thing you notice about a giraffe? Its l-o-o-o-ng neck, of course. Why would any animal need such a neck?

The giraffe shares its home with huge herds of other plant-eating animals, including zebras, rhinos, elephants and many kinds of antelope. Most of these animals feed on grasses and shrubs. Competition for food could get serious if these low-lying plants had to support giraffes as well. But the giraffe feeds mainly on the leaves and twigs of trees. With its super long neck and legs, it can reach even the top branches.

You may be surprised to hear that a giraffe's neck has only seven bones—exactly the same number as yours. These seven neck bones, or vertebrae as they are called, are simply much, much larger than yours—or any other animal's for that matter! The vertebrae also fit together with special "ball and socket" joints, allowing the giraffe to move its neck smoothly and gracefully.

"How's the weather down there?"

Multipurpose Necks

Giraffes are affectionate creatures and they like to hug each other—just as we do. Of course they do not have arms, so they "hug" by rubbing heads and necks. This is called "necking." It is usually done gently, but sometimes two male giraffes will get a little rough with each other—especially if they are interested in the same female.

Necking then becomes a show of strength, with the males swinging their heads and long necks like wrecking balls. A giraffe's head is quite light for its size, but a male who has had many head-butting battles grows extra layers of bone on his skull. Because of this his head may weigh up to 45 kilograms (100 pounds).

The battle between two males can become quite spectacular. Usually one giraffe—or both—tires after 15 or 20 minutes, and the encounter ends without any serious injury.

Neck to neck.

Overleaf:
Giraffes often serve as walking watchtowers for other animals.

On the Lookout

Thanks to its great height and its remarkable eyesight, the giraffe has an excellent view of its surroundings. Not only can it see over the top of many grassland trees, but the design and location of its eyes give it almost "wrap-around" vision. It can therefore see danger approaching from any direction with only a slight turn of its head.

Giraffes also have acute hearing and a keen sense of smell. No wonder zebras, antelopes and other animals often gather around them to take advantage of their superior lookout skills.

When watching for danger, two heads are better than one.

Getting Around

If you think it would be fun to take a giraffe for a walk, think again. Since a *walking* giraffe covers well over four metres (about 15 feet) with each stride, you would have to run all the way at top speed to keep up.

Giraffes have a very unusual way of walking. They swing both legs on one side of their body at the same time—both right legs, front and hind, then both left legs, front and hind. This way of walking is called *pacing*.

Walking is very definitely the giraffe's preferred way of getting around, but if danger threatens it can gallop at a speed of 50 kilometres (30 miles) an hour, swinging its back feet out together so that they land ahead of its front feet. Because of its size and weight, however, a giraffe cannot keep up this pace for long. As soon as it is out of danger, it slows down to a walk again.

On the move.

Watch that Kick!

Giraffes are peaceable creatures. They don't bother other animals and would rather run from danger than fight. But fight they can and will if attacked or provoked.

Actually, very few animals are foolish enough to attack an adult giraffe. Babies are a different matter, but a giraffe mother will fight fiercely to defend her young. Her powerful legs and dinner-plate-size hoofs are suddenly transformed into deadly sledgehammers, and a single well-aimed kick can kill a full-grown lion.

This comparison of hoof-prints will give you an idea of the size of a giraffe's hoof.

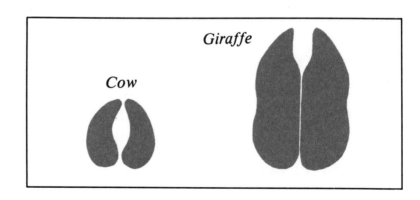

Cow

Giraffe

Only a desperately hungry lion or several acting together will attack anything as big as a full-grown giraffe.

Giraffe Talk

Giraffes are quiet by nature. Because they seldom make sounds, many people believe that they cannot. This is not true. Giraffes may bleat like sheep and snort or moan or moo like cows. They seem to reserve these sounds for extra special occasions, however, such as saying hello to a strange giraffe or greeting a possible mate.

Sounds are not a giraffe's only means of communication. Like many other animals, it also uses body language to let other giraffes know how it is feeling. An angry giraffe, for instance, lowers its head and neck straight out in line with the ground. And to end a fight with another giraffe, the loser will stretch its neck and point its nose skyward. This says, "I know you are boss!"

One of the giraffe's most obvious message-movements is running. This signals danger to other members of the herd and they will all follow immediately. One gallop says it all.

Sounding off.

Horns A-plenty

A giraffe has at least two horns on its head but some bulls, as the males are called, have even more—occasionally as many as five. These horns are an outgrowth of the skull, but unlike those you find on sheep or cattle, they are covered with skin and stiff hairs.

The giraffe is one of the few animals that is born with horns. At first, however, they are made up of softer, gristly material called cartilage. This gradually changes to real bone and becomes very hard as the giraffe gets older.

Although female giraffes, or cows, have horns too, only the males seem to put them to much use. In fact, one quick way to tell a male from a female is to look at their horns. The males usually wear the hair off the ends of theirs by using them when they battle each other to see who's stronger.

The Inside Story

If a giraffe's blood circulation system were just like yours, the poor thing would faint every time it lifted its head up from drinking. Fortunately, the giraffe's circulation system is specially designed for its unusually large size.

First of all, the giraffe needs a very strong heart and plenty of pressure to move the blood from its body all the way up that long neck to its head. With a heart weighing over 12 kilograms (25 pounds) and blood pressure twice that of a human, the giraffe's circulation system is perfectly suited to making sure blood reaches all parts of its body. Also, its veins and arteries are equipped with special trap doors to keep the blood from moving too quickly when the giraffe changes position.

A tree stump makes a handy scratching post for those hard-to-reach places.

Opposite page:

Up to one metre (3 feet) long, the tassel of coarse black hair on the end of the giraffe's tail is useful for swishing away flies and other insects.

Personal Patterns

Did you know that giraffes from different places come in different patterns? It's true. Scientists divide giraffes into nine groups based on what part of Africa they live in, their size and color patterns. Even they have trouble telling some of the groups apart, however.

The most easily recognized giraffe is called the Reticulated Giraffe after its pattern of sharply outlined dark patches. The word *reticulated* means "like a net," and that is exactly what the neat, narrow white lines of this giraffe's pattern look like.

The other eight groups of giraffes all come in some variation of a pattern type called *blotched*. Blotched patterns are much less clear and regular than the reticulated pattern.

Belonging to one particular group of giraffes does not mean that you look just like every other giraffe of that group. In fact, every giraffe has its very own arrangement of patches. Just as no one anywhere has fingerprints exactly like yours, no giraffe has spots that exactly match those of any other giraffe.

Tongue Twister

Just think how much ice cream you could get in one lick if you had a tongue as long as your arm! But where would you keep such a tongue when it wasn't in use? Fortunately, the giraffe—which does have a tongue about as long as your arm—has plenty of room for it inside its large head.

The giraffe's remarkable tongue is about 45 centimetres (18 inches) long, narrow, and blackish at the end. It is also very rough and muscular, and the giraffe can use it almost as delicately as you can use your hand. With its tongue, a giraffe can carefully pluck the leaves off even the thorniest tree or twist twigs over its sharp lower teeth to cut them off a branch.

Giraffes have 32 teeth, just like people. But there is one big difference—they have no top front teeth. Instead, they have a bony ridge up front and plenty of broad grinding teeth at the back which they use to chew up their food.

Who needs a knife and fork!

Bring on the Browse

As you may have guessed, giraffes eat a lot. They have to in order to keep their large bodies strong and healthy.

Giraffes are browsers, which means that they feed on twigs and leaves but do not usually eat grass. They spend many hours a day feeding. Bulls often eat 30 kilograms (66 pounds) of food a day and may eat even more. Acacia leaves are a giraffe's favorite food, but they also enjoy mimosa and wild apricot leaves.

Giraffes do not spend a lot of time drinking, and it is just as well they don't. Getting their heads down to water level is an awkward undertaking. It can also be a dangerous one as predators often wait at water holes to attack. Giraffes get most of the water they need from the leaves they eat, but when they do stop for a drink they may take in as much as 35 litres (9 gallons) of water at one time.

Being tall has its advantages—the giraffe can feed on leaves no other animal can reach.

Chew and Chew Again

The giraffe has a specially designed four-part stomach that allows it to get the most from the leaves and twigs that it eats. One part of its stomach also acts as a holding chamber.

A giraffe can eat its meal very quickly because it does not have to bother to chew much before it swallows. Later, when it is relaxing in a safe place, it brings the food back into its mouth to chew it thoroughly. What the giraffe brings back into its mouth is called cud. Other animals, such as deer, cows and camels, also chew their cud.

To avoid the heat of the midday sun, giraffes feed mainly in the early morning and evening.

Traveling Together

The giraffe weighs between 550 and 1800 kilograms (1200–4000 pounds). It takes a LOT of food to keep a body like that running efficiently. To find enough food the giraffe moves over great distances and has no fixed home.

Giraffes usually travel together in herds of 20 to 30 cows and calves. Most bulls travel alone and only join the herd for short periods of time for mating. If there is plenty of food in an area, a herd of 70 or more animals may gather.

Often, with small groups, there is a bull who seems to consider himself a kind of boss. The other giraffes are not too concerned with this, however, and are free to come and go as they like.

Giraffes do most of their traveling and feeding in the morning and evening when it is cool. They rest at night and during the hottest part of the day. A giraffe usually just dozes standing up, but it will occasionally lie down for a short nap, twisting its neck around to rest its head on its back.

What a Baby!

Giraffes can breed all year, although in some areas they do so only between July and September. If there is a herd bull, he will usually father the young, but a male from outside the herd often joins for this purpose. A battle may result, and this is important as it ensures that only the strongest males father the babies.

Fourteen months after breeding, the female gives birth to a single baby weighing 45–70 kilograms (100–150 pounds). The mother stands up while giving birth. This means that the calf has a long drop into this world. But baby giraffes are sturdy creatures. They have to be. Less than an hour after birth they are standing up nursing from their mother.

Feeding on mother's milk.

Giraffe Daycare

The baby giraffe stays alone with its mother for a time, and she does not allow it to mix with other giraffes very often. After a few weeks, however, she joins other cows to share the job of bringing up the babies.

The calves are collected together into a "nursery" where they stay quietly in the shade of trees. They are not allowed to go out into the open plain to feed. The cows take turns, one or two at a time, watching the calves while the other mothers are away feeding. The babysitters are very alert and are always on the watch for danger. Young giraffes are tempting to lions, hyenas and leopards.

The cows return several times during the day to nurse their babies and stay with them throughout the night.

Discovering the great wide world.

Saving Energy

Giraffe babies do play and run, but not nearly as often as other young animals. Instead they spend most of their early months lying peacefully in the shade watching the world around them.

This is important for two reasons. One is that giraffe calves need to protect themselves from losing water to the hot African sun. The other is that they need to save energy for the important task of growing up.

Since even lions are wary of tangling with a full-grown giraffe, growing up is the best protection from hungry hunters. And giraffes grow more quickly than any other mammal baby except the Blue Whale. They may grow over two centimetres (an inch) a day during their first week or two of life, and they almost double their height in the first year.

By the time it is 18 months old, this calf may be almost as tall as its mother.

Growing Up

The baby giraffe begins to nibble on leaves and twigs when it is two or three weeks old. It will need its mother's milk for many more months to come, but it must learn what to eat and how to eat it. The giraffe's tongue may be a very good tool for getting hold of plants and twigs, but it takes plenty of practice to make it work properly.

Under the watchful eyes of the adults the calf is well cared for. In a few months it will be ready to join its mother during her daily trips to feed. It will be completely independent by the time it is two years old and will be ready to be a parent on its own a year or two after that. With a little bit of luck, the young giraffe can look forward to 20 or even 25 years of roaming the vast African plains.

Words To Know

Breed To produce young.

Browse Young twigs, leaves and shoots of plants that animals feed on. Also to feed on these things.

Bull Male giraffe.

Calf Baby giraffe.

Cartilage In a young animal, firm rubbery tissue that gradually hardens into bone.

Cow Female giraffe.

Cud Hastily swallowed food brought back to the mouth for chewing by certain animals including deer, cattle, and giraffes.

Horns Outgrowths, usually permanent, from the heads of certain animals. In most animals, horns are covered with a hard, smooth material, but in the case of the giraffe, they are covered with skin and hair.

Necking Behavior of giraffes that consists of intertwining necks. Most often seen when two males are engaging in a test of strength.

Pacing A way of walking in which both legs on one side of the body are moved at the same time.

Reticulated Word meaning "like a net." Used to describe the pattern of one particular type of giraffe's coat.

Savanna Flat grassland of tropical or subtropical regions.

Vertebrae The individual bones that make up the spinal column.

INDEX

ancestors, 9

baby. *See* calf
blood circulation, 29
breeding, 41

calf, 6, 41, 42, 45
   size, 11, 41
   growth rate, 45
coat patterns, 30
communication, 25
cud, 37

defense, 22, 45
diet, 12, 34
digestive system, 37
distribution, 9
drinking, 34

enemies, 22, 34, 42, 45
eyes, 18

growing up, 45, 46

habitat, 9
head, 15
heart, 29
height, 11, 18
herd, 38

hoofs, 22
horns, 26

legs, 11, 12, 21
lifespan, 46
locomotion, 21

neck, 12, 15
necking, 15

okapi, 9
pacing, 21

relatives, 9
Reticulated Giraffe, 30

senses, 18
size, 11, 38
sleep, 38
social organization, 38, 42
speed, 21

tail, 30
teeth, 33
tongue, 33
travel, 38
types of, 30

weight, 38

Cover Photo: Tony Stone Worldwide (Masterfile)

Photo Credits: Bill Ivy, pages 4, 13, 24; Harvey Medland (Network Stock Photo File), pages 7, 16-17; The Globe and Mail, Toronto, page 8; FPG International (Masterfile), page 10; Freeman Patterson (Masterfile), pages 14, 39; Zefa (Masterfile), pages 19, 20; Len Pizzen, page 23; Tony Stone Worldwide (Masterfile), pages 27, 40; M. Mara (Valan Photos), page 28; George Calef (Masterfile), page 31; Metro Toronto Zoo, page 32; New York Zoological Society, pages 35, 36; Ron Watts (First Light), pages 43, 44.